4-8-75

# PROCLAMATION:

**Aids for Interpreting the
Lessons of the Church Year**

## HOLY WEEK

### SERIES B

*HOLY WEEK*

**William C. McFadden**
**and**
**Reginald H. Fuller**

FORTRESS PRESS                    Philadelphia, Pennsylvania

*Library of Congress Catalog Card Number 74-24932*

ISBN 0-8006-4074-8


4698C75      Printed in U.S.A.      1-4074

# General Preface

*Proclamation: Aids for Interpreting the Lessons of the Church Year* is a series of twenty-six books designed to help clergymen carry out their preaching ministry. It offers exegetical interpretations of the lessons for each Sunday and many of the festivals of the church year, plus homiletical ideas and insights.

The basic thrust of the series is ecumenical. In recent years the Episcopal church, the Roman Catholic church, the United Church of Christ, the Christian Church (Disciples of Christ), the United Methodist Church, the Lutheran and Presbyterian churches, and also the Consultation on Church Union have adopted lectionaries that are based on a common three-year system of lessons for the Sundays and festivals of the church year. *Proclamation* grows out of this development, and authors have been chosen from all of these traditions. Some of the contributors are parish pastors; others are teachers, both of biblical interpretation and of homiletics. Ecumenical interchange has been encouraged by putting two persons from different traditions to work on a single volume, one with the primary responsibility for exegesis and the other for homiletical interpretation.

Despite the high percentage of agreement between the traditions, both in the festivals that are celebrated and the lessons that are appointed to be read on a given day, there are still areas of divergence. Frequently the authors of individual volumes have tried to take into account the various textual traditions, but in some cases this has proved to be impossible; in such cases we have felt constrained to limit the material to the Lutheran readings.

The preacher who is looking for "canned sermons" in these books will be disappointed. These books are one step removed from the pulpit: they explain what the lessons are saying and suggest ways of relating this biblical message to the contemporary situation. As such they are springboards for creative thought as well as for faithful proclamation of the word.

The authors of this *Holy Week - Series B* volume of *Proclamation* are William C. McFadden and Reginald H. Fuller. Dr. McFadden, the editorhomiletician, is a member of the Society of Jesus and Associate Professor in the Department of Theology, Georgetown University, Washington, D.C. He is a graduate of Woodstock College, Woodstock, Md. (B.A.), Bellarmine College, Plattsburgh, N.Y. (Ph.L), and Fordham University, New York (M.A.). He studied theology at College St.-Albert-de-Louvain, Belgium (S.T.L.), in Muenster, Germany, and at the Gregorian University in Rome (S.T.D.). Dr. McFadden has served as chairman of the Department of Theology at Georgetown University since 1966. Much of his preaching experience comes from his association with Holy Trinity parish in Washington. Dr. Fuller, the exegete, is Professor of New Testament, Virginia Theological Seminary, Alexandria, Va. He is a native of England and a graduate of Cambridge University (B.A., M.A.). He served parishes in England and taught in colleges in England and Wales prior to coming to the United States in 1955. From 1955-66 he was Professor of New Testament Literature and Languages, Seabury-Western Theological Seminary, Evanston, Ill., and from 1966-72 he was Baldwin Professor of Sacred Literature, Union Theological Seminary, New York. Dr. Fuller is a prolific author and translator. His most recent work, which is directly related to this present volume, is entitled *Preaching the New Lectionary* (Collegeville, Minn.: The Liturgical Press).

# Table of Contents

# The Sunday of the Passion, Palm Sunday

| Lutheran | Roman Catholic | Episcopal | Pres./UCC/Chr. | Methodist/COCU |
|----------|----------------|-----------|----------------|----------------|
| Zech. 9:9-12 | Isa. 50:4-7 | Zech. 9:9-12 | Zech. 9:9-12 | Zech. 9:9-12 |
| Phil. 2:5-11 | Phil. 2:6-11 | Phil. 2:5-11 | Heb. 12:1-6 | Phil. 2:5-11 |
| Mark 15:1-39 | Mark 15:1-39 | Mark 14:32—15:39 | Mark 11:1-11 | Matt. 26:14—27:66 |

## EXEGESIS

*First Lesson: Zech. 9:9-12.* Chapters 9-14 of Zechariah consist of a collection of messianic prophecies quite distinct from the prophecies of the first part of the book. These latter chapters formed an important quarry for the primitive church in its search for material for its passion apologetic, an apologetic which sought to answer the questions: Why should Jesus have suffered? How, if he suffered, could he be the Messiah?

Today's reading combines two quite distinct messianic prophecies. The first (vv. 9-10) pictures the messianic king as a man of peace, whereas in vv. 11-17 he is depicted as a warrior. By stopping at v. 12 our selection plays down this contrast and allows us to read vv. 4-11 in the light of Jesus' entry to Jerusalem on Palm Sunday and vv. 11-12 in the light of his redemptive death ("my blood-of-the-covenant," Mark 14:24) on Good Friday. It thus covers both the minor (except for the Pres./UCC/Chr. Ch. lectionary, where it is the sole theme) and major theme of this day. In v. 11b the captives were for the original author the exiles in Babylon after 586 B.C. In the Christian interpretation they stand for all men under the bondage of sin. The stronghold (v. 12a) in the original text meant the earthly Jerusalem. In the Christian interpretation it becomes the heavenly Jerusalem, the kingdom of God.

The Roman Catholic selection (Isa. 50:4-7) is the second of the four servant songs, which recurs in sequence in Wednesday in Holy Week and is commented upon there.

*Second Lesson: Phil. 2:5-11.* This passage occurs every year and so was commented upon in *Proclamation* last year. For many reasons vv. 6-11 are

1

regarded by most contemporary exegetes as an early Christian hymn which the apostle has utilized and commented upon. The immediate context is an exhortation to humility (v. 5). Among the reasons for supposing that the hymn is pre-Pauline we may note its rhythmic character, its concern with basic kerygmatic affirmations, the large number of un-Pauline words (this disposes of the common British view that it was a hymn composed earlier by the apostle himself) like "form," "equality," "a thing to be grasped," (or, as we should translate it, "a thing to be clung to"), "in human form," "highly exalted." Note, too, that the apostle continues to quote from the hymn after it has ceased to be relevant to his immediate purpose: he passes beyond the humiliation of the Christ to his exaltation.

Despite the general agreement that it is in verse form, the division of the hymn into lines and stanzas is much controverted and affects the interpretation. Some divide it into two stanzas and interpret the first stanza to refer exclusively to the earthly life of Jesus, the second to his exaltation. We prefer a four-stanza division which would yield the pattern pre-existence and incarnation—incarnate life—exaltation—final triumph:

I

(Christ Jesus) who though he was in the form of God
did not regard equality with him a thing to be clung to,
but emptied himself
and took a bond-slave's form.

II

So he was born like any other man
and in his human mode of existence
he humbled himself
and became obedient to death (yes, a death on a cross).

III

Consequently God exalted him higher (than all the powers)
and gave him the name
which is above every name,

IV

that in the name of Jesus
every knee should bow
and every tongue confess
"Jesus is Messiah and Lord."

In this four-fold division stanza I covers the pre-existent life of the Redeemer as the divine Wisdom, enjoying a mode of existence like that of God himself. Wisdom, however, did not cling to this status, but divested itself of it and became incarnate in Jesus, being subject like all men to the onslaughts of the powers of evil. Stanza II: in this human mode of existence, however, the incarnate wisdom reversed the human situation by refusing to succumb to the powers (unlike Adam) and lived a life of complete obedience maintained to the point of death (Paul adds as a gloss, that this death was a death on a cross; for the cross is not merely the exit of wisdom from this world and its return to eternity, but the culmination of the incarnate One's obedience). Stanza III: the exaltation and enthronement of Christ affirm the efficacy of the incarnate One's obedience and death on a cross; they do not cancel them out or relegate them to the past. Stanza IV: the final goal of his enthronement is that the exalted One should be acknowledged by all the cosmic powers as Messiah and Kyrios, universally recognized for what he has become as a result of his obedience unto the death of the cross.

Heb. 12:1-6 (Pres./UCC/Chr. Ch.) contains in summary form the same christological pattern of humiliation/exaltation, but develops the parenesis in a different direction. Instead of an exhortation to humility, it leads into an exhortation to perseverance and endurance. Hebrews envisages a community or a group within a community which has become bored and tired with the Christian life.

*Gospel: Mark 15:1-39.* Since the form of the passion story is that of a continuous narrative rather than a series of isolated units strung together, it does some violence to its literary form when only a section of it is read. Note that the Episcopal reading runs from the arrest to the death; that is the earliest form. Later the narrative was extended backward to start from the plot of the Sanhedrin (Mark 15:1). The episodes covered in today's selection are: the trial before Pilate, the release of Barabbas, the mockery, the *via dolorosa*, the crucifixion and accompanying incidents, the death of Jesus, and the centurion's confession. The passion narrative, though it allows the outline of the story to be reconstructed, was designed primarily to express the following kerygmatic truths: (1) that Jesus died as Messiah; (2) that he died for our sins; (3) that he died in accordance with the scriptures (1 Cor. 15:3-4). Of these points (1) is expressed in the trial scene and in the *titulus*; (2) does not figure in the body of the narrative but is confined to the cup word at the supper (a restraint that increases our confidence in the historicity of the main outline); (3) is expressed in a number of details in the passion story (the wine mingled with myrrh, the dividing of the garments, the cry from the cross, etc.) It is always a moot point whether the OT prophecies have created the particular incident or whether the incident has led to search for the prophecy. But these considerations affect the peripheral details, hardly the central core of events. This basic outline may be summarized as follows: Jesus was sentenced to crucifixion by the Roman authorities, to whom the Jewish authorities had handed him over as a messianic pretender. He carried his cross to the scene of his execution (Simon of Cyrene is probably adduced as an eyewitness, his two sons being known very likely to the community where Mark wrote). There Jesus was executed with two criminals (perhaps Zealot guerrillas), and died a premature death. Thus far we have noted the original history and its development in the tradition. Finally there is the evangelist's redaction. This can be seen in the wording of the centurion's comment on Jesus' death: "Truly, this was the Son of God." The christological title, Son of God, plays an important role in the structure of Mark. It occurs (probably, though the text is uncertain) at Mark 1:1, at the baptism, and at the transfiguration. In the first part of the Gospel it remains a secret known only to Jesus himself and the demons. It is disclosed to the inner group of disciples at the transfiguration but they are silenced until after the passion. Then it is finally revealed to the Gentile centurion at the foot of the cross. Mark is telling his readers that Jesus can be confessed as Son of God only as the crucified One. To call him Son of God does not mean that (as people were saying in Mark's church) he was merely a miracle worker or "divine man," i.e., an epiphany of the divine. The title refers not to Jesus' "divinity" considered as an abstraction, but concretely to the saving act which God has wrought in him.

## HOMILETICAL INTERPRETATION

In the gospel narrative of the passion, first the story of Jesus is told, then the teller of the story gives his comment. It is suggested in today's exegetical notes that Mark's comment on Jesus' death is contained in the cry wrung from the lips of the centurion: "Truly, this was the Son of God."

The homilist may profitably dwell on this process since it is the same sort of process which is taking place between him and his hearers. Like the evangelist he is telling the story of Jesus and adding to it his own comment. It is of paramount importance that he not overlook this aspect of his role in the liturgy. He is not simply to bear the Book in solemn procession and read from it to his congregation. He is not simply to explain some difficult passages. He must make his own personal comment on the sacred text. He must take a position with respect to it. He must also point out to his hearers that they are under the same obligation of adding their personal comment to the biblical word (and to the word of the homilist!). Only in this way are they truly hearers of the word.

There is, of course, another possible order. When the readings are very lengthy, or when for any other reason less time is available for the homily, it can be a very effective move for the homilist if he makes some remarks *prior* to the reading of the sacred text. This serves to orient the mind of the listener to certain key ideas and helps him to hold together a long reading.

In fact, even on ordinary days this method may open up the word of God so that it speaks directly and with added power to a congregation which has in this fashion been prepared ahead of time to hear it. Too often congregations are forced to sit patiently through readings which they cannot easily follow. This puts the homilist in the position of having to explain the texts before proceeding to the homily itself.

The selection from Philippians is a good example of a homilist taking the story of Jesus and applying it to the lives of his people. Paul is writing to a church he dearly loved. He wanted them to do all in their power to remain united with a common purpose and a common mind. That, he tells them, is the one thing that would make him completely happy. He wanted them to avoid self-glorification and conceit. They were to think always of the good of others first. That is how Paul pictured life in the ideal Christian community.

How was he to motivate them to this self-forgetful way of living? His answer is to take the story of Christ and focus on the first part of it, the downward movement that begins with the exalted state of the pre-existent Christ, proceeds through various stages of humiliation, and finally climaxes in his pitiable death on the cross. This whole downward movement was not thrust on him. He chose it. Though enjoying equality with God, he emptied himself out completely and utterly. This self-emptying disposition is characteristic of the mind of Christ Jesus and the Philippians are exhorted to put on this same mind and let it re-fashion the way they live with one another.

Today's reading from Zechariah weaves together two messianic themes, the greatness of the royal descendant of David and the lowliness of the One through whom Yahweh brings about salvation and universal peace. The result is a strong paradox which is only intensified by employing these verses on Passion Sunday. At the beginning of the solemn commemoration of Jesus' final days on earth, we are invited to rejoice and shout with gladness. A king arrives in Jerusalem. He is triumphant and victorious. And yet he does not ride in on a warlike steed, but on a simple donkey, and his victory in war is a victory over war. By passing through war he establishes peace.

The acceptance of Jesus on Sunday with waving palm branches and hosannas is contrasted sharply with the rejection he received a few days later. It is worth noting that it is not simply a case of Jesus having to undergo suffering. You can suffer as a hero, receiving great admiration and support. The rejection robs his passion of any halo of earthly glory. It is suffering without honor. The cross means death as a despised reject. Those like Peter who refused the whole notion of his being destined to suffer grievously (Mark 8:33), ended up fleeing into the night, leaving him alone. This is not the kind of Lord they wanted.

This is suggestive of the various paradoxes of the passion: Jesus walks through sorrow to attain the joy of heaven, experiences rejection to enter into glory, endures suffering to come to eternal rest, undergoes death to pass over to life.

These paradoxes have become too familiar to our ears. We need someone to help us feel again the sense of shock at the reversal of human standards they embody. Only in a flow of words does someone glibly pass "through death to life." If a homilist can properly evoke the reality of death, its darkness, its helplessness, its apparent finality, he may re-awaken in us the sense of this mystery of faith: how strange and unlikely that this should lead to that, that the path to death is the path to life!

In evoking a sense of the reality of death, the homilist may find some help in Tom Stoppard's play *Rosencrantz and Guildenstern Are Dead*. In it the leader of an acting troupe remarks that the only kind of death audiences believe in is melodramatic stage death. One time an actor in his troupe was condemned to hang for stealing a sheep so the leader got permission to have him hanged during the play. It was a disaster. The man just was not convincing. He did nothing but cry all the time. The audience jeered at him and threw peanuts, but he just stood there and cried.

Rosencrantz observes that there must have been a moment when it first became clear to each of us that we were not going to live forever. It must have been a shattering moment, one that is stamped indelibly in one's memory—and yet he cannot recall it. Maybe we are born knowing we are going to die, or maybe we cannot allow ourselves to realize that fact.

The exegetical notes recall the problem of the early Christian apologetic: If Jesus suffered, how could he be the Messiah? We are not dealing here with a simple paradox, but with a grave scandal. How can this be the Messiah?

The scandal continues to our day. We are too used to the idea of a suffering Messiah to feel the original scandal. Perhaps another scandal strikes closer to home for us: If Jesus is the Messiah, if he is the one foretold by Zechariah, then what of the promise that "the bow of war will be banished"? If he is the one to proclaim peace for the nations, why do wars still rage and grow in virulence? Why do we live under the present possibility that one mad day of war could obliterate mankind from the face of the earth?

The homilist should face this scandal squarely, or better locate the proper source of the scandal. It is not so scandalous that God's anointed one should suffer and thus enter into his glory. It is not so shocking, to use the imagery in today's second reading, that one who was in the form of God should give up that exalted rank and take the form of a slave, or even that he would humble himself, obediently accepting death on a cross. The real scandal is that we have been so monumentally slow to heed the admonition Paul attaches to these words: "Your attitude must be Christ's." The truly shocking thing is that we are so persistent in refusing to act like people who have been redeemed, whose lives have been purchased at such a great price.

The second reading in the Pres./UCC/Chr. Ch. lectionary is the solemn climax in a litany of heroes of faith. The author of the Epistle to the Hebrews is trying to exhort his readers to perseverance in the face of difficulties. His strategy is to go through the list of biblical ancestors who in one way or another make his point: "Only faith can guarantee the blessings that we hope for, or prove the existence of the realities that at present remain unseen" (Heb. 11:1). He invokes the memory of Abraham and Jacob and Moses and so many others. "These were men who through faith conquered kingdoms, did what is right and earned the promises. They were weak people who were given strength to be brave in war and drive back foreign invaders" (Heb. 11:33-34).

Jesus is the final example, the one who is our leader in faith and who brings faith to perfection. There is a very significant phrase used here, which gains added force by reading this passage on Passion Sunday, as we stand at the beginning of Holy Week. The author does not simply exalt the quality of Jesus' faith, or praise his courage in putting up with the opposition of his enemies. We read that Jesus endured the cross "for the sake of the joy which was still in the future" (Heb. 12:2).

This recalls the parable of the man who found a treasure hidden in a field and who with great joy goes off and sells everything he owns in order to possess it (Matt. 13:44). The joy he looks forward to is so great he thinks nothing of giving up all he owns to possess it.

The homilist may choose to use this theme of joy to set a tone for the whole of the passion. All the heroes of faith were persons who drew strength and courage from a joy they hoped for. The victory they reached for was still unseen but they were firm in their conviction that it would be theirs.

So Jesus, as he enters the time of his passion, is fortified by faith to remain firm. But his faith gives him strength and courage because it is an unshakable conviction of the joy that is in his future according to the promise of the faithful God.

# Monday in Holy Week

| Lutheran | Roman Catholic | Episcopal | Pres./UCC/Chr. | Methodist/COCU |
|---|---|---|---|---|
| Isa. 42:1-9 | Isa. 42:1-7 | Isa. 42:1-7 | Isa. 50:4-10 | Isa. 42:1-9 |
| Heb. 9:11-15 | | Heb. 11:39—12:3 | Heb. 9:11-15 | Heb. 9:11-15 |
| John 12:1-11 | John 12:1-11 | John 12:1-11 or Mark 14:3-9 | Luke 19:41-48 | John 12:1-11 |

## EXEGESIS

*First Lesson: Isa. 42:1-9.* The first four verses of today's reading form the first servant song (the other songs, all read this week, are 49:1-6; 50:4-9; and 52:13—53:12).

The servant songs raise two main problems: (1) Their origin. Were they by Deutero-Isaiah himself, were they earlier compositions, or were they subsequent additions to the text? They stand out clearly from their surrounding context. It is most likely that Deutero-Isaiah took them over as preformed materials since he offers his own comments on them, and these comments are consistent with his theology as a whole. (2) Who is the figure of the servant? Many suggestions have been made. Those who think that he is an individual figure identify him variously with the prophet himself, with some other prophet, with a historical Hebrew king of the past, or with a future messianic king. Others regard the servant as a corporate symbol standing either for Israel as a whole, or for an ideal remnant. The trouble is that the servant songs seem to differ among themselves as to the individual or corporate character of the servant. Whatever the servant's original identity, for Christian faith the figure of the servant comes ultimately to rest in Jesus of Nazareth. There is still one remaining problem. Did Jesus in his lifetime identify himself with the servant? Did he take it as the inspiration or blueprint for his mission? Such was the prevailing opinion until quite recently. Now the identification is seen to be rather the result of the christological development of the post-Easter church—very early, but still not the earliest Christology. Read consecutively (and for this reason it is regrettable that the Pres./UCC/Chr. Ch. lectionary has departed from the consecutive order) the four servant songs cover the career of Jesus from his baptism to his death and subsequent vindication.

The first servant song (Isa.42:1-4) speaks of the servant's call and his endowment with the Spirit for his role in salvation history (v. 1). It then proceeds to characterize his activity (vv. 2-4a) and the goal of his career (v. 4b). The pre-Marcan tradition already saw v. 1 as a model for narrating Jesus' baptism and Matthew later saw in vv. 2-4a a prophecy of his ministry (Matt. 12:18-21) as characterized by the messianic secret. It is the whole preceding ministry of Jesus, from his baptism to his arrest, his proclamation of the inbreaking of God's eschatological reign, his call of the disciples to follow him, his eating with the outcasts, his exorcisms and healings, that provide a structure and meaning for the cross. There were hundreds of crosses in first century Palestine. This cross is different. It has saving significance only because of Jesus' prior self-understanding and his activity which expressed his self-understanding and intentionality. That is why this first of the servant songs comes fittingly on the first weekday of Holy Week.

The Pres./UCC/Chr. Ch. reads the third servant song today. For comment see Wednesday in Holy Week.


*Second Lesson: Heb. 9:11-15.* This is the core of the central argument of Hebrews, which runs from 7:1—10:25. Point by point the author builds up his case for the use of "high priest" as a title for Christ and as a framework in which to describe his redemptive work. In doing so he has provided a point by point comparison of the two priesthoods, Christ's and the Levitical. Now he sums up his conclusions in a succinct declaration. Christ as high priest entered once into the holy place, i.e., into heaven, taking with him his own blood, his life surrendered unto death. The effect of his work is to secure for mankind an eternal redemption, further defined as purging our conscience from dead works (=sins), to serve (the Greek word for "serve" is a cultic word, meaning worship) the living God.

The importance of this passage is that it indicates that the redemptive work of Christ upon the cross, his sacrifice, is a work which is of abiding efficacy. It is a work, as the writer so strongly emphasizes, which was accomplished "once for all" in a decisive moment of the past. Christ still applies his atoning for us and our salvation. Charles Wesley based one of his great eucharistic hymns on this passage:

O thou before the world began
Ordained a sacrifice for man,
And by the eternal Spirit made
An offering in the sinner's stead;
Our everlasting Priest art thou,
Pleading thy death for sinners now.

Thy offering still continues now
Before the righteous Father's view;
Thyself the lamb forever slain,
Thy priesthood doth unchanged remain;
Thy years, O God, can never fail,
Nor thy blest work within thy veil.

The Episcopal selection is less weighty doctrinally (Heb. 9:11-15 occurs on Wednesday). It consists of the conclusion of the great passage on the OT heroes of the faith and the exhortation to look to Jesus (see Pres./UCC/Chr. Ch. Second Lesson for Passion Sunday).

*Gospel: John 12:1-11.* On the Johannine dating the anointing takes place the Saturday before Holy Week. In Mark-Matthew it takes place early in Holy Week, hence its use today. This story presents a tangled series of problems in synoptic relationships and in the history of tradition. It exists in no less than three different forms in the Gospels (Mark-Matt., Luke, John). Here we can only say that in our view the Johannine version is independent of the other two but that there has been an intertwining of traditions of two basically different stories. John's version, like Luke's, represents a combination of the story of a penitent woman who wetted the feet of Jesus with her tears and wiped them with her hair, and a quite different story of a woman who anointed Jesus.[1] Several different interpretations of these actions have been given in the various traditions. In John the following interpretative motives are apparent: (1) The great extravagance of Mary's action. This extravagance is indicated by the statement that the fragrance of the ointment filled the whole house. The suggestion that this is an allegorical expression of the universality of the gospel (Hoskyns) is not convincing. (2) The theme of the poor is accentu-

---

1. See R. E. Brown, *The Gospel according to John*, Vol. 1 (New York: Doubleday, 1964), *ad loc.*

ated by the intervention of Judas. (3) The nuancing of the theme of Jesus' burial by the curious statement that the woman is to keep "it" (the ointment?). If so, how could she perform this extravagant act?

The real problem is, what did the evangelist intend by including the story of the anointing at this point? The only place where his hand can be clearly traced is in the cross-reference to Lazarus in vv. 1-2 and in the identification of Mary with Lazarus' sister. Clearly for him the anointing has some connection with that episode. Is it just that the same people and the same locale are involved, or is it some theological connection between the raising of Lazarus and the anointing? Probably the latter. The evangelist is telling us that the Jesus who raised Lazarus from the dead was in that very act proclaimed to be the resurrection and the life precisely because he was also the one whose day of burial was at hand, the one whom they would not have with them always as they would have the poor. Therefore Jesus is the resurrection and the life only because he himself died and was buried, and so glorified.

The Episcopal alternative Gospel reading (Mark 14:3-9) is the Marcan version of the anointing. Note that this version is uncontaminated by the other story of the penitent woman who wetted the feet of Jesus with her tears and wiped them with her hair. The two motifs of the poor and the anointing for the burial appear here and are again traditional. The Marcan redaction is to be seen in v. 9 (there is a growing consensus that the word "gospel" in Mark is always redactional). Mark is saying that the woman's action, pointing as it does (according to the tradition) to the burial of Jesus, calls attention to an essential aspect of the gospel. Jesus is not just a divine man or wonderworker. He is the crucified one whose crucifixion is constantly re-presented in the kerygma, and along with it the woman's action as a witness to his burial.

The Pres./UCC/Chr. Ch. Gospel reading (Luke 19:41-48) is the continuation of the Lucan version of the Palm Sunday entry (chosen for today despite the fact that the *Marcan* version was the Pres./UCC/Chr. Ch. reading yesterday). It consists of two episodes, Jesus' weeping over Jerusalem and the cleansing of the temple. Both emphasize that Jesus comes to Jerusalem to fling down the gauntlet of his final challenge to his people at the center of the national and religious life. This—rather than any theological purpose (e.g., to die as an atoning sacrifice)—was the historical intention of Jesus in his last journey to Jerusalem.

## HOMILETICAL INTERPRETATION

Today's texts reflect various attempts to find language to express the mystery of the passing over of Jesus to his Father.

The passage from John's Gospel focuses on the body of Jesus, which the evangelist has earlier described as the sanctuary of the new temple (2:21). The anointing of Jesus' feet is a foreshadowing of the preparation of his body for burial, the last sorrowful gestures with which his loved ones will consign him to the grave. There is sadness in Jesus' words, sadness not because of foreseen suffering, but because of the coming separation from those he loved. Those who watched him in action and heard his words knew of his deep affection for the poor. But this is not the time to think of their needs. These are his last days with them: "You will not always have me" (12:8).

In such a critical time Mary knew the right thing to do. This is the same Mary who on another occasion was praised by Jesus for having chosen the better part when she sat down at his feet and listened to him, and let her sister Martha bustle about in the kitchen doing less important things (cf. Luke 10:38-42).

The Episcopal alternate reading is Mark's account of the anointing of Jesus at Bethany. The woman is not identified as Mary and she pours the precious ointment over Jesus' head (not on his feet, as in John). Jesus' speech is somewhat longer, and emphasizes the extraordinary sensitivity of the woman to the significance of the moment. Though others became indignant over the waste (in Mark Judas is not the culprit) and were upsetting her with their grumbling, the woman had followed her heart. She took ointment worth nearly a year's salary and poured it all out in a gesture of unrestrained generosity. Jesus sides with her against the others. Her open-handed giving was closer to his heart than the prudent calculation of the other possible uses of the ointment. He is moved to declare solemnly that her story will be remembered wherever the gospel is proclaimed.

The homilist may wish to explore this point further. Why will her story be remembered wherever the gospel is proclaimed? How is it that in an account of the mighty works of God worked through his Son Jesus this small incident is raised to such prominence?

One possible answer is that this woman recognized what the others had failed to perceive: Jesus' presence was not a permanent possession which they could deal with in their own way and in their own good time. It was a gift offered to her then and there for an immediate response.

If this is the case, then she is remembered as an ideal of discipleship. Consequently, the question about giving the money instead to the poor should be seen in a different light. No special importance should be attached to Christ's words about the poor being always with us. The care of the poor is really not at issue here. It rather takes its place as one of many reasons men come up with to refuse or postpone the giving of themselves completely to Christ.

One man wishes to go and bury his father first (Matt. 8:21). Another man wishes to say goodbye to his people at home (Luke 9:61). In the parable of the great banquet Jesus describes the same pattern. The invitation goes out from the great king and the excuses come back: "I have bought a piece of land and must go see it. . . . I have bought five oxen and am on my way to try them out. . . . I have just got married and so am unable to come" (Luke 14:18-20).

The glory of this woman is that she seized the moment and responded to it fully. Putting aside the normal considerations of prudence, ignoring the disapproval of others, she celebrated the gift of Christ's presence, holding back nothing. We need her story. For this her story will be remembered wherever the gospel is proclaimed.

The identification of Jesus as the suffering servant in the Book of Isaiah was a particularly effective way in which the early church gave expression to the mystery of Christ. Today's passage helps to illuminate further the significance of Jesus' death. We are led to consider Good Friday not as a single great act of sacrifice but as the culmination of Jesus' life, growing out of the logic of all that had gone before.

Just as the servant is chosen by God and endowed with his Spirit, so Jesus begins his ministry by being baptized and receiving the Spirit from heaven (Mark 1:10). Jesus' entire ministry is conducted under the influence of the Spirit.

The mission of the servant is described as one of deliverance: the eyes of the blind are to be opened. So, too, are the doors of prisons and dungeons. John will describe the mission of Jesus in similar terms: he is the light of the world (8:12) and opens the eyes of a man born blind (9:1 ff.). Those who believe in him will know the truth and the truth will set them free (8:32). There is an echo here also of Luke's description of the day when Jesus read at a synagogue service in Nazareth those powerful lines from Isaiah:

> "The Spirit of the Lord has been given to me,
> for he has anointed me.
> He has sent me to bring the good news to the poor,
> to proclaim liberty to captives
> and to the blind new sight,
> to set the downtrodden free,
> to proclaim the Lord's year of favor" (61:1-2)

Here the homilist may choose to explore the implications of Christian baptism with its anointing of the new Christian to strengthen him in undertaking the same mission of bringing liberation to those who are unfree.

The author of Hebrews explores another image to bring out the mystery of Christ, the image of Jesus as the high priest of a new covenant. He has a special purpose in mind, however, and it is one which makes his words particularly appropriate for us. He is addressing a group of Christians whose situation is like ours today. They are trapped in a mood of discouragement and of disillusionment. Their earlier hopes have lost their vitality. Their certain expectation of deliverance by the coming of the Lord has become smothered under a mountain of doubts. They have lost their zest for a life lived in the service of God. Their actions seem to them "dead."

The form of Hebrews is that of a homily, but the homilist is faced with a group of people who are indifferent to the word of God. They radiate to him an attitude which says, "Preacher, it's all been said before many, many times for many, many years, and we still find ourselves in a very difficult situation, prey to fears and doubts, wondering if there is any point in coming to church anymore" (cf. 10:25).

The biblical author's strategy is to try to re-awaken hope in their hearts by showing that in Christ, the new high priest, we have access to God. The same Christ who offered himself in sacrifice to God has been established by God as the mediator between God and his people.

Christ lives before the Father, always interceding for us (7:25), so that we may be confident in approaching the throne of grace (4:16), and we may have hope through the prayer of Christ to have our spirits renewed. This very day he can "purify our inner self from dead actions" (9:14), and restore to our lives the sense that we are living them in the service of the living God.

The homilist may wish to undertake the formidable task of doing for his congregation what the author of Hebrews attempted to do: meet the challenge of indifference in the congregation to the Christian message. The categories of high priest, sacrifice, mediator, etc., may not be sufficiently forceful for his purposes. The basic need, however, of both groups may really be the same: to have a living experience again of the *presence* of God in their lives, of his fatherly interest in them, and thus a renewed sense that what they are doing really does matter.

In the Pres./UCC/Chr. Ch. lectionary the first reading today is the third servant song from Deutero-Isaiah, which is commented on in the notes for Wednesday of Holy Week. The Gospel reading is taken from Luke and the homilist should situate this text for his listeners as it fits into the theological program of Luke.

Jerusalem is the center of Jewish religious life and Luke begins his narrative with events which center around the temple, including the presentation of Jesus at the temple (2:22 ff.) and the visit of Jesus to the temple when he was twelve years old (2:41).

From that time on Luke never records any visit of Jesus to Jerusalem, but describes his ministry in such a way that it represents a gradual movement toward the holy city which brings together the growing interest of the people in Jesus and the rise of hostility towards him. The exegetical notes say that Jesus comes to Jerusalem finally in Luke to fling down the gauntlet of his final challenge. But, as he does so, Luke presents us with the touching picture of Jesus weeping over the city, lamenting over the fate of the city which he knew would not recognize the message of peace he was bringing.

It is good to have this image in mind as we continue through the events of the passion. In its own way it gives us an insight into the heart of Jesus as his ministry comes to its climactic phase, the confrontation in Jerusalem. It is a poignant picture of a gentle prophet who loved his Father and his people and foresaw the failure of his attempts to bring them together and the consequent ruin that would befall this beloved city.

# Tuesday in Holy Week

| Lutheran | Roman Catholic | Episcopal | Pres./UCC/Chr. | Methodist/COCU |
|---|---|---|---|---|
| Isa. 49:1-6 | Isa. 49:1-6 | Isa. 49:1-9a | Isa. 42:1-9 | Isa. 49:1-9a |
| 1 Cor. 1:18-25 | | 1 Cor. 1:18-31 | 1 Tim. 6:11-16 | 1 Cor. 1:18-31 |
| John 12:20-36 | John 13:21-30, 36-38 | John 12:37-38 42-50 | John 12:37-50 | John 12:37-50 |

## EXEGESIS

*First Lesson: Isa. 49:1-6.* This is the second of the servant songs. The additional verses, 7-9a, included in the Episcopal and Pres./UCC/Chr. Ch. readings, are not part of the song, but the beginning of another prophecy in which the nation's plight in exile is contrasted with the glorious times which will follow upon its restoration.

A unique feature of the second servant song is its explicit identification of the servant with the people of Israel (v. 3). This identification, however, by no means clears up the problem of identity in the other songs. For "Israel" could mean one who as an individual embodies and represents either the whole people (e.g., the king or the messianic king, or perhaps even a prophet), or the true remnant of the people. In any case, Christians can read this song, like the others, in terms of Jesus and his mission. In the NT it is used only once christologically (in the song of Simeon, Luke 2:32) and twice of the apostolic ministry (Gal. 1:15; Acts 13:47). The song itself contains no direct reference to suffering, and the addition of vv. 7-9a from the other prophecy supplies this lack in a reading for Holy Week. The song's main theme is the universality of the servant's mission (vv. 5-6), a mission for which the servant has been destined from his mother's womb (v. 1b). This is why Isaiah 49 is more usually associated with the epiphany season in Christian usage rather than with Holy Week. However,•the accompanying Gospel Lesson from John 12 ties up the theme of universality of the servant's mission explicitly with the cross, a link lacking in the Roman Catholic gospel reading.

*Second Lesson: 1 Cor. 1:18-25.* This section is the opening part of Paul's reply to the Corinthian problem described in v. 12, the tension between the various groups in the community. This reply extends from

1:18 through 3:23. (The Episcopal selection runs through the second paragraph, in which Paul gives a concrete illustration of the general principle he has laid down in vv. 21-25 in the first paragraph.) The Corinthian parties (not just one of them; all the parties are equally under attack) are priding themselves on their wisdom. They were probably influenced by an early form of gnosis (we follow the practice of distinguishing between first century gnosis and second century gnosticism, reserving the latter for the developed gnostic systems of the later period). They thought that man's basic need was not a redemption of the whole man but the knowledge of his true self. For Paul, man's fallenness is total and his need of redemption much more radical. He requires not information but transformation. Hence Christ came not to bring gnosis, not information about man's true being, but complete transformation. Hence too the necessity of the cross. The cross is "folly" to those who are unaware of their radical fallenness. If all man needed was information, the cross would have been unnecessary and meaningless, a stumbling block for the Jews and folly to the Greeks. Paul contrasts two programs for man's salvation, the gospel ("word," v. 18, and "kerygma," v. 21) on the one hand, and "wisdom of this world," (v. 20), on the other. In defining the gospel here exclusively in terms of the cross, Paul is not excluding other aspects of the saving event. The cross epitomizes the whole saving act of God in Christ which includes the sending of the Son (Gal. 4:4), his whole observable history, his whole career (what elsewhere Paul calls *sarx,* flesh) and his resurrection-exaltation (see the summary of the kerygma in 1 Corinthians 15 and the hymn in Phil. 2:6-11). The cross would not be a saving act if God had not first sent his Son, and its efficacy would not continue into the present as the saving act of God if it were not for the resurrection-exaltation, which alone makes the cross a present word of salvation. The wisdom of this world which Paul condemns is not the enterprise of philosophy as such. Christian theology has always been dependent upon philosophy for its terminology and conceptuality and often for the issues to which it has responded. Philosophy has always been the handmaid of theology. What Paul condemns is the existential attitude that registers itself in particular philosophies, the illusion that man can discover the ultimate truth about himself and so save himself, not needing an act of God to save him. The cross, however, is perceptible as the saving act of God only to the eye of faith ("who believe," v. 21), only to those who are being saved (v. 18), who are called (v. 24). This involves predestination. Insight into the saving significance of the cross as the power and wisdom of God (v. 24) is the gift of God. Yet, those who are perishing, those who do not see in the cross the saving act of God, blind themselves by their own choice.

*Gospel: John 12:20-36.* This passage is a collection of materials derived from different sources and representing different forms of tradition. It falls into three main sections: (1) vv. 20-22; (2) vv. 23-33; (3) vv. 34-36.

(1) Vv. 20-22. These verses must at one time have served as an introduction to an earlier pericope, probably as the setting for a pronouncement story. But the original pronouncement has been lopped off, and in its place a Johannine one substituted. The Greeks never see Jesus and drop out of the picture. The evangelist intends the real answer to the request to be found in the discourse.

(2) Vv. 23-33. Here are several items. V. 23 is a Son of man saying evolved in the Johannine tradition out of the primitive parousia sayings (note the word "glorify," derived ultimately from Dan. 7:14).

V. 24 is a parabolic saying, with good claim to be authentic.[1]

V. 25 is a saying about losing one's life to save it, a Johannine variant of the similar synoptic saying. It was evidently combined with the parabolic saying prior to the composition of the Fourth Gospel in order to interpret the parabolic saying. The principle of dying in order to produce fruit is the principle of the Christian life.

V. 26 is a variant of the synoptic saying about discipleship. It further interprets the parabolic saying, relating the life of discipleship to Jesus' passion.

Vv. 27-30 are a variant of the Gethsemane story. It is characteristic of the evangelist's procedure to place episodes from the passion story at an earlier point in his Gospel. Placed here, it elaborates further the passion theme already broached in the preceding verse.

V. 31 is a saying rooted in the apocalyptic tradition of the primitive church. But it has been modified by Johannine language ("of this world") and the future eschatology of the primitive church has been transposed into the present. "Now" is the judgment, "now" is the ruler of this world to be cast out. Note, however, that the "now" is not the now of Jesus'

1. See Dodd, *Historical Tradition in the Fourth Gospel* (Cambridge: University Press, 1963), pp. 266-67.

revelatory discourses in the earlier part of the Gospel, but the now of his passion. All that Jesus was revealed to be in the discourses he became concretely in the hour of his passion.

V. 32 is also a saying rooted in earlier tradition, namely, in the primitive Christian proclamation of Jesus' exaltation and in the proclamation of the universal efficacy of his atoning death (Mark 10:45; 14:24). But the saying has been developed in the Johannine school: the verb "draw" is characteristically Johannine and may be due to gnostic influence (Oepke). V. 33 is a typical Johannine redactional note both in form and in content. It explains that exaltation refers to Jesus' lifting up on the cross.

Here we have the response to the Greeks' question. They cannot see Jesus until he has been lifted up on the cross. Only then can the Gentiles gain access to his saving presence. Thus the theme of the whole pericope is the universality of God's redemption in the cross of Christ. It is the fulfillment of the universal mission of the servant of Yahweh (First Lesson).

(3) Vv. 34-36. It would have made the commentators', the preachers', and probably the hearers' task easier had the pericope ended with the great pronouncement in v. 32 and the appended comment of the evangelist. For the ensuing sayings develop a rather different line of thought. Indeed, Bultmann, who resorted to wholesale rearrangement of the text, attached these verses to John 8:29. V. 34 takes up the theme of the lifting up of the Son of man, but in terms derived more from 8:28 than from 12:32. Jesus' answer to the crowd's question looks a bit of a *non sequitur*, and forces upon his hearers the urgency of decision in view of the challenge of his revelation. The dualism light/darkness has some connection with the hour of the cross, but its main reference is to the dualism of decision which permeates the Johannine discourse material.

There is considerable variation between the lectionaries of the four traditions at this point. The Roman Catholic selection (John 13:21-30, 36-38) comprises the unmasking of Judas and the prediction of Peter's denial. The Episcopal reading (John 12:37-38, 42-50) and the Pres./UCC/Chr. Ch. (John 12:37-50) form the conclusion of the first half of John's Gospel, the signs and discourses. It consists of a testimonium from Isaiah 6, bringing to a climax the challenge to decision presented in the discourses and summarizing the teaching of the revelation discourses. This material seems less directly related to the theme of the passion than the Roman Catholic and Lutheran readings.

## HOMILETICAL INTERPRETATION

Today's readings suggest a sort of drama being enacted by God and those he has chosen. There is the divine call and man's response, a divine mission and man's labor. Then man falls into discouragement and God's response, strangely enough, is to extend his mission further. This does not discourage man but rather makes him aware that his thoughts are not God's thoughts and his ways are not God's ways. Man is moved therefore to put aside his fears and to trust completely in God.

The suffering servant of Isa. 49:1-6 is confident of his call and had been looking to become the one in whom God would be glorified. But his mission seems to him a failure and he asks himself, "Where is the glory of God that I hoped to see?"

Then God speaks to him in his grief and despair. The word is scarcely what the servant expects to hear. The servant is thinking, "I have toiled in vain, I have exhausted myself for nothing," and God says to him, "I have even greater plans for you. For I plan through you to bring all mankind to salvation."

The despair lifts and the servant comes to realize he has been judging by too human standards. There was no need for discouragement. "All the while my cause was with Yahweh, my reward with my God. I was honored in the eyes of Yahweh, my God was my strength" (vv. 3-4).

The story of Paul manifests striking similarities to that of the servant. The Lord makes his claim on the young Saul on the road to Damascus and after suitable preparation sends him on the mission of preaching the gospel. Paul is zealous in undertaking this apostolate, but regularly encounters opposition, persecution, or indifference. He finds himself unequal to the task, only to hear the Lord tell him, "My grace is enough for you; my power is at its best in weakness" (2 Cor. 12:9). So Paul makes it his special boast that he is weak, for then he is strong with the power of Christ. In the same way in today's second reading Paul boasts of the foolishness of the message he is preaching. For him that is a sign that God is at work.

Paul seems to have perceived a pattern in God's dealings with men. God regularly chooses the weak to overthrow the strong, the foolish to confound the wise. He calls Abraham out of his homeland and sends him to an unknown land without posterity and with no hope of having any, with the extraordinary promise that he will raise up from him a great nation. The infant Moses is marked for death, but is saved to become the leader who will free Israel from captivity in Egypt. Gideon is chosen to drive the Midianites out of the promised land, though he is the lowest member in his father's house and in the weakest clan in all Israel. When he raises a force of 32,000 men the Lord directs him to reduce the force until only 300 remain (Judg. 7:1 ff.). In this way it will be evident that it is the power of the Lord which is delivering Israel. Likewise, the young David went out against a heavily armed Goliath, taking with him only a slingshot and five smooth stones (1 Sam. 17:40).

Paul has perceived how regularly God challenges human wisdom and overturns human expectations. In this way God is calling us to listen for *his* word. Mostly we tell him what he may say to us. Like the Greeks we are looking for a wisdom which is like the wisdom we already have. Like the Jews we are looking for signs, but we want signs which confirm us in our present way of acting. Who of us is prepared to find the wisdom of God and the power of God in the broken, dying body of a man hanging on a cross?

The selection from the Fourth Gospel continues in its own way the same theme as the first two readings. Since Jesus is presented in this Gospel as already possessing, even in his life on earth, some share of his heavenly glory, we do not meet here a scene such as the agony in the garden, which would most closely approximate the picture given of the suffering servant as the suffering man of faith. The equivalent scene in John is in 12:27, where Jesus acknowledges that his soul is troubled.

Today's theme is present in the Gospel selection through the word that some Greeks wish to see Jesus, which is John's way of introducing the universality of the mission of Jesus. The whole world will only come to see Jesus, however, when he is glorified. Glorification comes in a way men could never dream possible: if Jesus is lifted up from the earth on a cross, he will draw all men to himself. John tries to soften the shock to our sensibilities by giving an analogy from nature. Why should we find it so strange that more abundant life comes out of death? After all, look at what happens in nature. If a grain of wheat falls on the ground and dies, it yields a rich harvest. Otherwise it remains alone.

In the concluding verses to this section of the Gospel, vv. 37-50, we read of the unbelief of so many Jews who acted out of fear. In their case it is fear of the Pharisees, or fear of being expelled from the synagogue. We have similar fears that keep us from coming to full belief. But perhaps the best formula for summing up our various fears is the one contained in 12:25. The man who clings to his life loses it. Let this stand for all of the fears that would close us off from the grace of God. Let it stand for the fears of the good men: of the suffering servant who thought all his labors were in vain and who doubted he would see the glory of God, of Paul who feared that his weakness would bring about the failure of his mission, and of Jesus himself whose soul was troubled as the hour of his passion came upon him.

And let it stand for the fears of other men, of people we know so well, who cling to their lives with both hands, afraid to let go. When Christ is lifted up, we are told, he will draw all men to himself—but not those men who fear death in all its forms, not only the death of the body but each day's little deaths of sacrifice, of loss of money or pleasure or comfort, and especially the difficult death of dying to oneself.

The man who clings to his life has all he can do to protect himself from the erosion of time and the encroachments of others. He must be careful, too, to keep under control the claims and demands of love. Such a man cannot afford to hear a divine call or undertake a divine mission. He cannot place all his trust in God or his faith in the love of another. He cannot "see" Jesus, even if Jesus is lifted up on the cross, or rather, especially since Jesus is lifted up on the cross. He cannot feel himself drawn by the example of such a life of unreserved giving. And so he loses his life.

The Pres./UCC/Chr. Ch. lectionary includes an exhortation made by Paul to Timothy. This selection may lead the homilist to develop some of the richness contained in the theme of light.

In 1 Tim. 6:16 God is said to dwell in inaccessible light, i.e., light symbolizes in this way the transcendence of God, "whom no man has seen and no man is able to see." Cf. also 1 John 1:5: "God is light; there is no darkness in him at all."

More commonly, light serves as a symbol of revelation or of the one who brings the truth. So John's Gospel speaks of the Word of God as "the true light that enlightens all men" (John 1:9).

In the story of the passion, though, it becomes especially clear that John does not picture darkness as an absence of light patiently waiting for illumination. Darkness is a power which is locked in a struggle with the light. When Jesus says in today's Gospel selection, "I, the light, have come into the world" (John 12:46), the context does not imply a serene manifestation of truth. As the exegetical notes today indicate, the main reference of the light/darkness dualism is to the dualism of decision. Thus Jesus continues by saying that his presence brings the conflict to the point of life or death. Whoever believes in Jesus escapes from the power of darkness. If a man rejects Jesus, he remains the captive of darkness. But a man cannot ignore him. He must choose.

Faith, then, is a struggling against the darkness, and Paul picks up this same theme with his exhortation to Timothy to "fight the good fight of the faith" (1 Tim. 6:12). At the time of his baptism Timothy made a profession of faith and spoke up for the truth in front of many witnesses. Paul here seems to suggest that this baptismal testimony is best understood in terms of the great profession of faith made by Jesus. Paul may be thinking specifically of Jesus' testimony before Pilate, when he proclaimed he had come into the world to bear witness to the truth (John 18:37), or more generally of the testimony Jesus gave throughout his entire passion. It matters little since these both are parts of a single testimony which came forth in a time of great struggle when Jesus resolutely decided to undergo the baptism wherewith he had to be baptized (cf. Mark 10:38). This suggests that Christian baptism is to be understood not so much as a permanent acquisition of truth as a taking sides in a continual struggle against a hostile power.

The Roman Catholic Gospel selection concerns the Lord's foretelling of his betrayal by Judas and of Peter's denial. Homiletical reflections on these two topics may be found in Wednesday's section.

# Wednesday in Holy Week

| Lutheran | Roman Catholic | Episcopal | Pres./UCC/Chr. | Methodist/COCU |
|---|---|---|---|---|
| Isa. 50:4-9a | Isa. 50:4-9a | Isa. 50:4-9a | Isa. 52:13-53:12 | Isa. 50:4-9 |
| Rom. 5:6-11 | | Heb. 9:11-15, 24-28 | Rom. 5:6-11 | Rom. 5:6-11 |
| Matt. 26:14-25 | Matt. 26:14-25 | John 13:21-35 or Matt. 26:1-5, 14-25 | Luke 22:1-16 | Matt. 26:14-25 |

## EXEGESIS

*First Lesson: Isa. 50:4-9a.* This is the third servant song. Here we may speak for the first time of the suffering servant. Here, too, the servant is much more clearly an individual figure than was the case with the second song. Three things are said about the servant, all of which find their fulfillment in the history of Jesus. First, the servant receives day by day a message from Yahweh to pass on to his hearers. He has first to hear the word himself before he can speak it to others. This picture of the servant's inner life corresponds remarkably to the portrait of Jesus in the Fourth Gospel. In the Johannine discourses Christ says "I have given them the words which thou gavest me" (John 17:8). He says, too, that after he has been glorified the Jews will learn the secret of his authority: "then you will know that I am he, and that I do nothing on my own authority but speak thus as the Father taught me" (John 8:28). Second, the fact that he declares to the world the word he has received from Yahweh involves the servant in rejection and suffering (v. 6). This reminds us that in the Gospels the death of Christ is not an absurd, irrelevant end to a life which had quite a different meaning, as Bultmann portrayed it in his book *Jesus*, but is absolutely integral to it, the climax of his ministry as the servant of God.

The Pres./UCC/Chr. Ch. reading (Isa. 52:13—53:12) will receive comment under Good Friday.

*Second Lesson: Rom. 5:6-11.* Paul's plan in chaps. 5-8 of Romans was apparently to outline the kind of life made possible for those who have been justified by the grace of God alone through faith, a case which he had argued in 3:21—4:25. He starts off in 5:1-5 to describe his life but his restless mind causes him to return again and again to the saving event which made this new life possible. This pericope is just such a reversion. Having spoken in v. 5 of the love of God, he expounds precisely what is meant by love. (1) Vv. 5-8 stress its completely unmerited character. (2) In v. 9 he reverts directly to the subject of the previous chapters, but this time under the same rubric of love. God's love in Christ is his act of justification. This is very important. Too often, we take the love of God as an abstract quality which must be reconciled with the harsh realities of life: How could a God of love allow this or that to happen? In the NT, however, the love of God is his act of justifying us in Christ. It is often forgotten that Charles Wesley's hymn, "Jesus, lover of my soul" is all about justification. (3) The saving event is described under the image of reconciliation (v. 10) which—and here Paul returns to the Christian life—is an occasion for rejoicing.

For the Episcopal reading (Heb. 9:11-15, 24-28) see above, Monday in Holy Week.

*Gospel: Matt. 26:14-25.* Once again, on formal grounds it is not entirely satisfactory to isolate part of the passion narrative in this way, since with one or two exceptions, like the institution of the Lord's Supper, the passion narrative is continuous. However, today's Gospel reading covers part of the prelude to the narrative proper. It consists of three paragraphs: (1) Judas' plot to betray Jesus; (2) the preparation for the passover; (3) the unmasking of Judas. Clearly the role of Judas (paragraphs one and three) occupies the center of our attention today. The preparation for the passover serves here to provide the setting for the unmasking of Judas. We are not concerned at this time with the Last Supper as such. Our modern curiosity is very anxious to know what motivated Judas to betray Jesus. The NT has no such interest. Any answers we give to that question are inevitably speculative. Perhaps the most plausible conjecture is that Judas was somehow infected with Zealotism and because Jesus did not fit in with his program he sought to get rid of him. But we shall never know. For the early Christian community the problem of Judas lay elsewhere: How could God allow such a thing? The early Christians were convinced that everything that happened in Jesus' passion happened by the foreknowledge and predetermined counsel of

God. They sought to alleviate the scandal of Judas by searching the (OT) scriptures. Hence we find the assertion that "the Son of man goes as it is written of him" (v. 24). Surprisingly, Matthew does not seek to elucidate his Marcan *Vorlage* as he so often does, and we are left wondering what scriptures the text has in mind. It is fairly certain that the passage in mind was Ps. 41:9 (cf. RSV margin): "Even my bosom friend in whom I trusted, who ate of my bread, has lifted his heel against me." Note, however, that the reference to God's will as declared in scripture does not relieve Judas of responsibility: "woe to that man . . ." Here we touch once more (see Second Lesson) upon the mystery of God's foreknowledge and man's free will. Both have to be held together in tension and paradox. God has foreknowledge and we have free will. God uses man's sin to overrule the consequences of his deeds for his own good purpose. *O felix culpa!*

The first alternative in the Episcopal selection (John 13:21-35) covers much of the same material as the Roman Catholic selection for Tuesday. Most of it is the Johannine version of the unmasking of Judas. But in John the theodicy question is ignored. Here is the bold assertion that Judas acted as the agent of Satan.

The Pres./UCC/Chr. Ch. reading (Luke 22:1-16) begins with the parallel Lucan account of the compact of Judas. But it diverts attention from Judas by running on into the first part of the actual supper narrative, a questionable procedure since vv. 15-20 form a single block of pre-Lucan tradition.

## HOMILETICAL INTERPRETATION

The readings for Wednesday may be viewed as unfolding in climactic fashion the special quality of Jesus' death.

The first reading is the third of the servant songs. The pattern is one that is familiar. The servant hears the word that the Lord addresses to him. When he preaches that word, he creates opposition. Like the prophets before him, he is subjected to persecution. He does not fight back but trusts in the Lord, who finally does come to his aid. His enemies will all fall to pieces like a moth-eaten piece of cloth.

Paul in the second reading fastens on a remarkable aspect of Jesus' death. We are no longer in the pattern of the third servant song. Despite certain similarities the whole thrust of the action is radically different. Christ died, we are told, not simply in fidelity to his mission of preaching. Christ died *for* men—helpless, sinners, enemies of God, men in no sense deserved such an extraordinary demonstration of love. Paul goes a step further. The fact that Christ died for us while we were still sinners is not only a sign of Christ's love for us. It is proof that God loves us.

Paul gives a picture of the redemption which is utterly removed from that of an angry God who demands retribution and who is moved to pity by the sufferings of Christ. On the contrary, it is out of his love and compassion for sinful men, who have set themselves up against him, that the Father sends his own Son to save mankind. The Son willingly accepts this mission despite the suffering and rejection it entails. God further pours out the Holy Spirit on men's hearts to bring them back into union with him. Given this reaching-out on the part of God to save mankind, the redemption would only be frustrated if God's enemies were destroyed.

The Gospel selection for today focuses our attention on the figure of Judas Iscariot. Perhaps in so doing it heightens dramatically a very special dimension of the love Jesus showed in his passion. For Judas is not simply a sinner, one among many whom Christ came to save. Nor is Judas simply one of those who rose up in opposition to Jesus and his mission. Judas is the one who is referred to as "the traitor." (Matt. 10:4; Mark 3:19; Luke 6:16).

There is a special shrug reserved for dismissing the traitor, the man whose malice consists in profiting from violating a trust. An opponent can be respected, but the man who betrays a trust can never be trusted again.

Judas is one of the intimates who shares with Jesus his final meal. They both dipped bread into the same bowl. He was entrusted with the common purse and, John tells us, he was a thief and used to help himself to the money that had been given to Jesus (John 12:6). When he decided on his act of treason, we find again the desire to turn this act to his own profit: "What are you prepared to give me if I hand him over to you?" (Matt. 26:15).

The betrayal finds its culmination in Judas' choice of a way to identify Jesus in the darkness of Gethsemane: "The one I kiss, he is the man. Take him in charge" (Matt. 26:48).

It is worthwhile to dwell a moment on this scene. Jesus has just been through the long and difficult agony in the garden. Now he must face one of his chosen twelve, who comes up to him and singles him out for arrest with greetings and a kiss.

In Mark's Gospel Jesus does not respond to Judas. But Luke and Matthew wish to give some expression to Jesus' response to Judas. In Luke Jesus says, "Judas, are you betraying the Son of man with a kiss?" (Luke 22:48) Matthew records the words, "Friend, do what you are here for" (Matt. 26:50).

It is tempting to see in the expression "friend" a demonstration of Jesus' abiding affection for one of his close followers, even in the act of betrayal. This is surely what comes across in respect to Peter's denial.

Perhaps the word, though, does not bear that meaning. It only occurs three times in the NT, and all three are in the concluding pages of Matthew's Gospel (20:13; 22:12; 26:50). The first instance is in the parable of the vineyard laborers. Those who had been working all day grumbled at the landowner for paying the latecomers as much as them. His answer is, "Friend, I am not being unjust to you," etc. The second instance is in the parable of the wedding feast where the king notices one of the guests is not wearing a wedding-garment and questions him, "Friend, how did you get in here without a wedding-garment?"

In both these instances the speaker has been subjected to some provocation and, while he continues to speak courteously, he is pointing out his dissatisfaction with the other man's conduct. This suggests that Matthew does not wish to make the point that Jesus continued to show affection to his betrayer. Perhaps there is some irony in the use of the word "friend," and surely a great deal of sadness at being so used by one he had trusted.

But the meaning of Jesus' reply is best found in the words which follow: "do what you are here for." Matthew is underlining the fact that Jesus has come through his agony in the garden. He has resolved what his course of action must be. He is being betrayed by one of his close friends. No matter. No more than it matters that "all his disciples deserted him and ran away" (v. 56).

The Jesus we see here is not a weak and submissive man, someone being carried away, helpless before larger forces. We see instead a man so strong and fixed in his resolve to drink the chalice of suffering according to his Father's will that he has no time to concern himself with the betrayal of Judas or the desertion of all of his disciples. The end is coming and he goes forth to meet it alone.

If the homilist is interested in pursuing the story of Judas, the picture unfortunately becomes very unclear. Still, it may be profitable to explore it.

The Acts of the Apostles contains a tradition that Judas purchased a field with the thirty pieces of silver and that he fell, apparently by accident, and died there (Acts 1:18-19). Matthew, on the other hand, relates a different tradition. On learning that Jesus had been condemned, Judas repented of his deed. He took the pieces of silver back to the chief priests and confessed, "I have sinned. I have betrayed innocent blood." Then, flinging the coins into the sanctuary, he went out and hanged himself (Matt. 27:3-6).

A comparison with Peter is unavoidable. Just a few verses earlier in his Gospel Matthew described Peter's triple denial of Jesus, which culminated in Peter's calling down curses on himself and swearing, "I do not know the man." The cock crowed at that moment and Peter remembered that Jesus had foretold his denial. Peter then went outside and wept bitterly (Matt. 26:69-75).

Why do these men react so differently to their sin? There may be a salutary lesson here. Judas, we read, repented of his deed. He confessed his sin. He rid himself of his ill-gotten money. What did he lack? Why was he unable to turn back to Jesus? One is tempted to speculate that it is because he is turned in on himself. His repentance is not productive of forgiveness because it does not even lead him to ask for forgiveness. "*I* have sinned. *I* have betrayed innocent blood." Is there an accent here that comes from deeply wounded self-esteem? When a person cannot tolerate the fact that *he* has sinned, he often uses the expression, "I cannot forgive myself for what I did." If someone is locked up this way inside himself, it is impossible for him to turn and ask forgiveness of another.

Peter, however, follows a different course. He wept bitterly, but his sorrow does not prevent him from coming to receive forgiveness. One indication that Peter was not caught in a paralyzing self-recrimination is that the story is preserved for everyone to know. Far from suppressing all trace of his denial as incompatible with his growing importance in the early church, the record of his weakness forms a permanent part of the preaching of the good news and enters into the composition of the NT. It is as if Peter does not wish to forget it, and wants us to benefit as well from its being remembered. It is an unforgettable testimony to the weakness of man and the mercy of God.

Perhaps the best comment on these two men can be found in some words of Paul. In a previous letter to the Corinthians Paul had caused them some distress, but their sorrow led finally to repentance, and this is the kind of sorrow God approves of. While not thinking of Peter and Judas, Paul's words are most appropriate: "The wound which is borne in God's way brings a change of heart too salutary to regret; but the hurt which is borne in the world's way brings death" (2 Cor. 7:10 NEB).

# Maundy Thursday

| Lutheran | Roman Catholic | Episcopal | Pres./UCC/Chr. | Methodist/COCU |
|---|---|---|---|---|
| Exod. 24:3-11 | Exod. 12:1-8, 11-14 | Exod. 12:1-14a | Deut. 16:1-8 | Deut. 16:1-8 |
| 1 Cor. 10:16-17 (18-21) | 1 Cor. 11:23-26 | 1 Cor. 11:23-26 | Rev. 1:4-8 | 1 Cor. 10:16-21 |
| Mark 14:12-26 | John 13:1-15 | John 13:1-15 or Luke 22:14-30 | Matt. 26:17-30 | Mark 14:12-26 |

## EXEGESIS

*First Lesson: Exod. 24:3-11.* Today we break the sequence of the servant songs (the fourth will be read tomorrow in all lectionaries except the Pres./UCC/Chr. Ch.). This reading comprises the inauguration of the Mosaic covenant. The narrative is composite: vv. 3-8 are from E, 9-11 from J. Moses enters into a book the words of Yahweh revealed to him on the mount (chap. 20), inaugurates the covenant by a blood sacrifice (vv. 4-5), throwing half of it on the altar and sprinkling the rest on the people (v. 8). By this rite the people are involved in the covenant. Vv. 9-11 are unconnected with this rite, and consist of a quite separate report of a theophany. The vision of God is consummated in "eating and drinking" (v. 11, a sort of communion rite). It is doubtless for this reason that the second paragraph is included in today's reading. We have here a double typology of the Lord's Supper: the inauguration of the covenant with blood and a participation of the people of God in that covenant by means of a communion meal. This typology has a biblical sanction, for Exod. 24:8b, "Behold the blood of the covenant," has shaped the cup word in the institution narrative at Mark 14:24.

The Roman Catholic and Episcopal reading from Exodus 12 is the institution of the passover. Since the Lord's Supper has a paschal background in the Marcan passion narrative (though not in the institution narrative itself) and in the Lucan Supper narrative throughout (including the institution narrative) this reading is quite appropriate for today. However, in Judaism it was used precisely at the passover rite itself, and this usage passed in early Christianity into the paschal liturgy (see, e.g., the passover homily of Melito of Sardis), so it would seem to belong more properly to the vigil services on Easter Eve. The Pres./UCC/Chr. Ch. reading (Deut. 16:1-8) is the Deuteronomic version of the institution of the passover. Unlike the exodus parallel, which comes from JE, the D account combines the two rites of the unleavened bread and the passover lamb. Both aspects of the meal play a role in Christian typology (1 Cor. 5:7-8), but in connection with the Christian passover celebration, not directly with the Lord's Supper.

*Second Lesson: 1 Cor. 10:16-17.* This is one of Paul's two *loci classici* on the Last Supper. The context of the present passage is as follows. Certain groups in the Corinthian community, probably influenced by early gnosis, thought they had already attained salvation. They therefore felt free to participate in pagan sacrificial meals with impunity. Paul, however, regards such practices as dangerous. Celebration of the Lord's Supper involved a *koinonia* (i.e., a communion participation, a term which implies a thoroughgoing sacramental realism, according to Conzelmann) in the body and blood of Christ. Participation in Christ is exclusive because it places one under obedience to the *Kyrios*. It can tolerate no participation in other cult deities.

To make this point Paul draws upon some traditional liturgical formulations. The "cup of blessing" is a Jewish phrase, meaning the cup over which the name of Yahweh is blessed (Jews did not bless things, but rather blessed Yahweh in thanksgiving for his gifts). Similarly, the phrase, "the bread which we break," did not symbolize the breaking of the Lord's body on the cross, an idea not found until later textual tradition in 1 Cor. 11:24 (see RSV margin). It was a purely utilitarian procedure necessary in order to have the common loaf distributed among all present so that they would be involved in the blessing said over it. Similarly with the blessing said over the cup. Paul would have regarded both individual wafers and individual communion cups as an unfortunate obscuring of the eucharistic symbolism! To these traditional phrases Paul adds his own questions, "Is it not a participation in the blood/body of Christ?" It is a striking fact that Paul here reverses the usual order of bread/cup, and some have thought that this represents an actual liturgical custom. This is not so. Paul is not citing a complete liturgical formula here, but only excerpts from such a formula, and he reverses the order because he wishes to comment at further length upon the bread part (v. 17). Elsewhere Paul follows the normal order of bread/cup (see 1 Cor. 10:3-4, and especially 1 Cor. 11:23-25, where he is actually citing the liturgical agenda of his communities). One further point before we leave v. 16. Body and blood are not things, stuff, but the one central event of salvation—the sacrificial death of Christ. The bread and wine are the body and blood of Christ in the sense of sacramental identification (Conzelmann) of one event (partaking of the bread/cup) with another (the saving event). The one event is brought out of the past and made contemporaneous with the other.

In v. 17 Paul makes further comment on the bread word. Partaking of the one loaf unites the participants into one body. The Lord's Supper has thus a horizontal as well as a vertical dimension. It involves *koinonia* with each other as well as with the Lord. But the horizontal dimension is created by the vertical.[1] The eucharist is not just a celebration of ordinary human togetherness.

The *koinonia* aspect of the communion was not in itself an original contribution of Paul to eucharistic thought. It was merely his comment on what the tradition already implied. Here he draws out what is implied by the *esti* ("is") in the bread and cup words of the traditional institution narrative and by the anamnesis formula (Do this for the recalling of me, as the passover was the recalling of the exodus salvation event). The further comment about the bread in v. 17 is, however, an original contribution. It was Paul who first gave a double meaning to the *Corpus Christi*. It is for Paul both sacramental and ecclesial, and the ecclesial depends upon the sacramental.

The Roman Catholic and Episcopal reading consists of the other *locus classicus* in 1 Corinthians (11:23-26), the institution narrative. Much of what we have said in our comments above relates also to this passage.

The Pres./UCC/Chr. Ch. reading (Rev. 1:4-8) consists of the initial vision of the exalted Christ in the Apocalypse. Presumably it is chosen today because of vv. 5-6 which speak of the saving event in the blood of Christ and the establishment thereby of the royal priesthood of the whole church.

*Gospel: Mark 14:12-26.* This pericope consists of part of the continuous passion narrative (vv. 12-21, 26), into which has been inserted at some stage of the pre-Marcan tradition the institution narrative (vv. 22-25). The

---

1. See Luther's profound remarks on *koinonia* given in J. Pelikan, *Luther the Expositor* (St. Louis: Concordia, 1959), pp. 191-204.

surrounding framework consists of: (1) the preparation for the passover (vv. 12-16), (2) the narrative of the supper in which Judas is unmasked (vv. 17-21), and (3) the exit to the Mount of Olives (v. 26). We regard the institution narrative as an originally separate tradition for the following reasons: (a) in 1 Cor. 11:23-25 Paul cites it as a separate pericope; (b) the Johannine passion supper narrative contains no institution; (c) the surrounding narrative presents the Last Supper as a passover meal while the institution itself ignores this point; (d) a particularly telltale piece of evidence is the repetition in v. 22 of the phrase "and as they were eating" from v. 18 as a peg on which to hang the institution. Therefore we conclude that the function of the institution is that of a separate aetiological cult narrative (i.e., it is concerned not to relate what happened at the Last Supper, but how the Marcan community was celebrating the Lord's Supper). Our commentary will concentrate on this narrative (14:23-25). It consists of three parts: (1) the actions and words over the bread (v. 23); (2) the actions and words over the cup (v. 24); (3) the eschatological saying (v. 25).

(1) The actions and words over the bread. The bread is *artos* (leavened), not *azuma* (unleavened). Mark's account presumes the ordinary weekly eucharist, not the annual Christian passover. Four actions with the bread are prescribed: taking, blessing, breaking, and giving, and a fifth implied (see the command "take" and cf. the statement that they drank of the cup). "Take" means lifting up the bread "a hand's breadth." It has nothing to do with the "offertory," as is often thought. That is only a preliminary to the taking. "Blessed" is a more primitive term than "gave thanks," which appears later with reference to the cup. For its meaning see the commentary on the Second Lesson above. The words over the bread are very brief: simply words of sacramental identification. An interpretative addition is not added as in 1 Cor. 11:24, "which is for you." In this respect Mark is more primitive than 1 Corinthians. Less primitive, however, is the dropping of the reference to the intervening meal (contrast "after supper" in 1 Cor. 11:25). In Mark's church both the bread and cup followed the meal.

(2) The actions over the cup correspond to those over the bread, except, of course, there is no breaking. The bringing together of the bread and cup rite through the removal of the meal between has resulted in assimilation of the bread and cup words: this is my body/this is my blood,

instead of: this is my body/this is the new covenant (1 Cor. 11:24-25). Here again Mark is less primitive, but it is still clear that blood means not the stuff but the saving event. In Mark, too, the cup word has to bear the whole weight of the covenant/atonement theology. The Pauline tradition identified the covenant with the new covenant of Jer. 31:31 ff. But in Mark the covenant saying is based on the typology of the Mosaic covenant in Exodus 24 (see above, First Lesson). It is now *my* blood-of-the-covenant, as opposed to the Mosaic blood-of-the-covenant. "Poured out for many" is tacked on awkwardly to the preceding phrase. The passive participle is a reverential periphrasis indicating that it is God who pours out the blood of his Messiah. The messianic sacrifice is the redemptive act of God (Jeremias). "For many," in accordance with contemporary rabbinic usage, does not mean "some but not all" but precisely "all"—all of the nations. The language is derived from Isa. 53:12. So the atoning, covenant theology has a double background, Exodus 24 and Isaiah 53.

(3) The eschatological saying has the highest claim to authenticity (Bornkamm, Schweizer), since the tendency in the history of the tradition is for the eschatological saying to become atrophied. Already in 1 Cor. 11:26 it is reduced to "until he comes" and finally in the later liturgies it disappears altogether. It contains implicitly all that is asserted in the bread and cup words about the Lord's Supper. "I will no longer drink" implies that Jesus will not, but they will. He is going to die, they will be left behind. The next time Jesus drinks wine, it will be in the consummated kingdom of God. This implies that the death of Jesus is the decisive event which lies between the Last Supper and the realization of the kingdom. Unfortunately, Mark does not add "with you" (Matt. 26:29), but it is apparently implied. Since the church continued to celebrate the eschatological meal in the joy of Christ's risen presence, it understood its rite as the fulfillment of Jesus' prediction at the Last Supper.

Mark contains no command to repeat (1 Cor. 11:24, 25 and Luke 22:19). But the very fact that form-critically Mark 24:23-25 is a cult aetiology (i.e., it gives the reason for the church's practice) is enough to indicate that the command to repeat is implied. And that it was done for the recalling of the Lord is indicated by the words of sacramental identification over the bread and cup.

The Roman Catholic and Episcopal Gospel reading (John 13:1-15) comprises the other main incident in the supper tradition, the foot washing (these lectionaries consider the institution of the eucharist sufficiently covered by the Second Lesson). This story has two levels of meaning. First, in the pre-Johannine tradition, it was an example of humility and service (cf. Luke 22:24-27). Second, in the Johannine redaction it became a piece of dramatic symbolism, expressing the total way of Christ: as he lays aside his garments, washes the disciples' feet, and resumes his garments, so he lays aside his eternal glory to become incarnate, stoops to redeem men throughout his humble incarnate life culminating on the cross, and then in the resurrection and exaltation resumes his heavenly glory.

The alternative Episcopal reading (Luke 22:14-30) is the Lucan account of the Last Supper. It should be read with the full text including vv. 19b-20 (RSV margin, Common Bible text). There has been a remarkable shift of text-critical opinion in recent years in favor of the long text and the RSV was undoubtedly wrong in relegating it to the margin. The long text is again aetiological: it represents the Christian passover as celebrated in Luke's church, with an initial cup breaking the pre-paschal fast, no lamb, and the Christian eucharist. The shorter text was produced by the puzzlement over the two cups at a time when the Christian passover was no longer celebrated in this way, and the church was familiar only with the weekly eucharist with bread and one cup.

The Pres./UCC/Chr. Ch. Gospel reading (Matt. 26:17-30) is the Matthean narrative of the Last Supper. It follows closely the Marcan version, but its institution narrative is more rubrical (Matthew was a churchman), placing the cupword during the drinking, not after as in Mark, and adding a further theological explanation to the word, "for the remission of sins" (v. 28; RSV: forgiveness).

## HOMILETICAL INTERPRETATION

There is a great deal of variety in the readings selected by the different churches for today.

The principal focus is to be found in the Gospel narration of the institution of the eucharist (Lutheran, Episcopal alternate reading, Pres./UCC/Chr. Ch.). The first and second readings mostly pick up the theme of blood, an enormously rich theme in terms of the Bible, but one which is hardly apt to prove rewarding to a congregation today. Perhaps the best the homilist can do is evoke something of its symbolic meaning to our ancestors in the faith.

The blood of the Mosaic Covenant, poured around the altar and sprinkled on the people, sealed a bond of union between them and God. The blood of the lamb, sprinkled on the doorposts of the Israelites, marked them as chosen people, as belonging to the Lord, and delivered them from the angel of death. So Jesus shed his blood as a way of bringing about union. His desire was to break down the barriers between God and his fellow-men, and to bring all men into a living harmony, delivering them from the power of death.

The Gospel reading in the Roman Catholic and Episcopal lectionaries deals with a distinct event at the Last Supper, viz., the washing of the feet of the disciples.

The homilist may choose to join both of these accounts by means of the notion of "prophetic action." Those who are preaching on the eucharist will find that the foot washing helps to interpret it, and those who are preaching on the foot-washing will find that this scene is illuminated in terms of the subsequent institution of the eucharist. For each of these two in its own way is a prophetic action which aims at revealing the meaning of Jesus' death on the cross. It finally comes down to this: What can it mean to me that this man was put to death outside of Jerusalem so many centuries ago?

We have, unfortunately, seen far too much of killings, executions, and assassinations. We find ourselves asking what these deaths mean. What significance should be attached to the killings of Martin Luther King, John and Robert Kennedy? What of the deaths of so many other nameless ones, whose passing was as unnoticed by our world as Jesus' death was in his?

A man's death may come suddenly, accidentally, and the meaning of it may be for us only this: the life of a man is a fragile thing. Or a man may be executed and the meaning of his death may simply be that superior force carried him away against his will and snuffed out his life.

But Jesus' death was not like that. In a variety of ways we hear Jesus saying, "I see this coming. I accept it—for your sake."

Let us look at some of the ways he tried to help us to see the meaning of his death. He did not use the method beloved of teachers. He did not give a lecture on the subject. He performed instead a couple of prophetic actions. We recall that at times the prophets engaged in symbolic actions that in their own way gave notice of what was to come and its meaning, e.g., by taking an earthenware jar and smashing it on the ground (Jer. 19:10-11) or by taking a cloak and cutting it into twelve pieces (1 Kings 11:30-31). What were these prophetic actions which Jesus performed to instruct us in the meaning of his coming death?

For one thing, he gave a dinner and invited his closest friends. It is difficult for us to place ourselves imaginatively in that scene but we should try. We are too accustomed to eucharistic services which may serve well as memorials of the Lord's death but bear no resemblance whatever to the Last Supper.

A college group once tried to recapture something of the atmosphere of the Last Supper by celebrating the traditional Jewish seder service during Holy Week. They invited a rabbi to be present but conducted the service themselves. The group was properly reverent. They said all of the prayers with a great solemnity. Finally the rabbi could not keep silent any longer. "You're much too stiff and formal," he said. "When we do it, we say a prayer, then talk or laugh a bit, then we have a glass of wine, and after some more conversation we say another prayer. It's a big family thing. If you people keep going the way you're going, you'll be done in twenty minutes."

So they did as he suggested and gradually began to enjoy themselves very much. The result was that the service lasted over three hours. If we wish to imagine for ourselves this dinner, we need to remember that these were friends gathered together to celebrate the passover.

Of course, this was not simply a passover meal between friends. Jesus did not act simply as a good host who provides food and drink to his guests. There is something special here and we must give it our closest attention, but we must keep in mind the setting Jesus chose in which to explain to his friends and to us the meaning of his coming death.

What is special is that at one point in this meal he took some bread and broke it and gave it to each one, and he took a single cup of wine and passed it to each one in turn. What is special is that the same food and the same cup are *shared*. He gave it to them.

How do I understand the meaning of the cross? How do I interpret the brute fact of his being put to death like so many hundreds of thousands of others in the course of history? I return to this picture of Jesus saying that this bread is his body and then breaking it and sharing it with his friends.

And I see him taking a cup and saying that it holds his blood which will be poured out as a sign of his love for his fellow-man. And I get the message that communion with him is sharing his way of dying.

All of us who eat of the one bread are called to live out the promise of unity with each other symbolized by the single loaf of bread we share. And all of us who drink from the cup of the new covenant should be moved by the example of our ancestors at Sinai who, when they had listened to the commandments of the covenant, cried out, "We will observe all that the Lord has decreed; we will obey" (Exod. 24:7). Sharing in the blood of the new covenant would be an empty memorial if we did not likewise pledge ourselves to observe all that the Lord has decreed and obey the new commandment that he gave us: "love one another; just as I have loved you, you also must love one another" (John 13:34).

There is a second prophetic action, the one described in the Roman Catholic and Episcopal reading from the Gospel of John, the washing of the feet. There are really two levels of meaning here. The first and basic one is that Jesus tells us that his death on the cross means that he submits himself to his death like a slave, like a servant who comes in to wash the feet of guests reclining at table, a man hardly noticed whose service is scarcely recognized. This humble obedience was very pleasing to his father.

The second meaning is in terms of the example he gives to the disciples. We could take this, as Peter seems to do at first, as the institution of a new ritual, a new rite of purification that the disciples were to repeat in his memory. It is interesting how little the church has made of the washing of the feet as a ritual. Perhaps this is because it was too clear from the beginning that it was not a ritual that Jesus had in mind. In a ritual the roles are already assigned, and carrying them out, even the role of a servant, can be an honorable thing.

No, Jesus did not have a new ritual in mind, and neither did he mean by his example that just as he has died for us, or washed our feet, so we should wash his feet or be ready to die for him. Think of the character in Camus' novel *The Fall*, whose friend is imprisoned and who therefore sleeps on the floor so that he may not have comforts which are denied to his friend. Jesus is not saying, "I have slept on the floor for you so you should sleep on the floor for me." His example is that he, being lord and master, has washed our feet and *therefore* we should wash each other's feet. There would have been something consoling about washing the feet of the Lord, but this is not the example he gave us.

And so this second prophetic action helps us to understand what happened on Calvary because it helps us to understand the spirit that moved Jesus to embrace his death. It helps us also to come to the conviction that, if we would have some share with him, we must live and go to our deaths not for him but, as he did, for our fellow man.

The Episcopal lectionary gives as an alternate reading Luke 22:14-30. The special material that is of interest here is that, immediately after the narration of the institution of the eucharist, Jesus in this account announces that one of those eating at that table was betraying him.

The disciples at once begin to ask one another who the traitor might be. In this context then we are startled to learn that a dispute arose between them about which of them was the greatest!

Jesus replies with what seems to us incredible patience. It is the same lesson he has been trying to communicate to them for a long time now. It is the lesson of his life and of his death. It is the same lesson that is contained in the prophetic action of the washing of the disciples' feet. Therefore, whichever lectionary he is following, the homilist may wish to introduce this material as well. It certainly does catch our attention and it is something we all have firsthand experience of: the desire to be reckoned as the greatest!

But it is this very desire which sets us against one another, which provokes disputes and dissension, and which, therefore, is diametrically opposed to the spirit of Jesus, the nature of his kingdom and the meaning of the eucharistic meal.

Jesus tells them that his kingdom is not modeled after those of pagan rulers. To be great is to act toward others with deference, and to be a ruler is to act as one who serves.

This is a very difficult lesson for men to learn. We have yet to do so. That may be why we find it difficult to grasp the spirit of Christ himself. It is so much easier to worship Christ and sing praises to his name. But how deal with the fact that he came among us as one who serves, and that he will not let us take him out of that role? Rather, as he serves us, he steadfastly insists that we learn the spirit that moves him, the spirit of the servant.

This is the lesson of his life and the lesson of his death. This is the teaching that is sacramentally present in the eucharist he gave us. As we learn it, we will come to know him, and will more joyfully assemble to celebrate the eucharist, and will become ourselves sacraments of Christ's presence in the world.

# Good Friday

| Lutheran | Roman Catholic | Episcopal | Pres./UCC/Chr. | Methodist/COCU |
|---|---|---|---|---|
| Isa. 52:13-53:12 | Isa. 52:13-53:12 | Isa. 52:13-53:12 | Lam. 1:7-12 | Lam. 1:7-12 |
| Heb. 4:14-5:10 | Heb. 4:14-16; 5:7-9 | Heb. 10:1-25 | Heb. 10:4-18 | Heb. 10:14-18 |
| John 18:1-19:42 (John 19:17-30) | John 18:1-19:42 | John 18:1-19:37 or John 19:1-37 | Luke 23:33-46 | Luke 23:33-46 |

## EXEGESIS

*First Lesson: Isa. 52:13—53:12.* Today we read the last and greatest of the four servant poems. It contains many problems of text, translation, and interpretation, but the general sense is clear. Whatever the precise identity of the servant (cf. first reading for Monday), he plays a crucial role in salvation history. Through him Yahweh brings the world to salvation through the knowledge of himself. In the process, the servant is rejected and humiliated, but God vindicates him, and those who had rejected and humiliated him come to recognize that he had suffered as an innocent victim and that by his sufferings their sins have been taken away.

The song falls into five parts (see RSV paragraphing). 52:13-15 forms an introduction, assuring us in advance that the servant will finally triumph despite his humiliation. 53:1-3 summarizes the sufferings of the servant. In vv. 4-9 the servant's tormentors acknowledge in the light of his vindication that his sufferings were vicariously undergone for their own sake, though they themselves inflicted them. Vv. 10-12 speak of the servant's vindication.

It is amazing how closely the fate of the servant corresponds to that of Jesus. The traditional view was that the prophet was predicting consciously and under divine inspiration the fate of Jesus. When this mechanical conception of prophecy was abandoned through the application of historico-critical methods to the OT, the view was substituted that Jesus himself consciously and deliberately modeled his own career on that of the suffering servant. Now that view in turn has broken down through the advance of tradition-criticism. The interpretation of Jesus in terms of the suffering servant (e.g., Mark 10:45; 14:25) is now seen as the result of early Christian attempts to understand the meaning of the Lord's death. From the earliest days after the first Easter his death was seen as having taken place in accordance with the Scriptures. At first Christians turned to Psalm 118 which gave them the interpretation of the Lord's death as the Jews' NO and the resurrection as God's YES. Later they hit upon Isaiah 53 and found there that the Lord's death was a vicarious atonement. Is the fourth servant song, then, nothing more than a quarry for early Christian theology? In what sense is it the word of God himself? We may understand it thus: the composer of the songs has a profound insight into the ways of God with man, and out of it he painted a picture which came to rest finally in the fate of Jesus of Nazareth. Hence Christian faith may in a very real sense read this fourth servant song as a song about Jesus of Nazareth, although that was not its original meaning. Texts do not have a static meaning through history. They acquire new meaning in the light of new events and experiences.

The Pres./UCC/Chr. Ch. substitute (Lam. 1:7-12) was apparently necessitated by the preemption of the fourth servant song for the Wednesday in Holy Week. Lamentations, traditionally ascribed to Jeremiah, consists of a series of poems bewailing the destruction of Jerusalem and the exile of the southern kingdom of Judah in 586. In Christian tradition the lamentations have been interpreted in terms of Jesus' passion, and readings from this book have been traditional in the office lectionaries in Holy Week from early times. Lam. 1:12 has a particular pathos for Good Friday, but it is not so theologically profound or as important for the *theologia crucis* as the fourth servant song.

*Second Lesson: Heb. 4:14—5:10.* The procedure of Hebrews is to follow a theological exposition by an exhortation. As we have seen, its major theological theme is the high priesthood of Christ. For this theme the author builds up his case gradually, enunciating it several times before developing it fully in the central section. Having first stated the theme at 3:1, the author now introduces it again, and this time expands on it by showing that Jesus had some of the necessary qualifications to be a high priest. His primary qualification was the sharing of our common humanity. He thus knew what temptation was and therefore is able to sympathize with our weaknesses (4:15) and to deal gently with the ignorant and wayward (5:2). The second qualification for a high priest is divine appointment; he must not put himself forward for the job. That this is true of Christ is proved from Pss. 2:7 and 110:1. Both Psalms 2 and 110 were used in the primitive church as testimonies for the resurrection. The author attaches particular importance to Melchizedek. He is concerned to show that there is another, eschatological high priesthood, distinct from the Aaronic priesthood. Unless there were another order of high priesthood it would not have been possible to claim high priesthood for Christ. The true Christ is like the Aaronic priest in some respects. He is human, was called by God, and appointed from among men. He was tempted as we are, is able to sympathize, offers a sacrifice. But in other ways he differs significantly. He is without sin (which has a positive rather than a negative meaning: Jesus committed himself totally to obey the will of his Father, Heb. 10:5-10). He was "made perfect," i.e., he achieved the goal for which he was appointed, and became the author of salvation. Yet, being truly and fully human, he had to learn obedience by overcoming temptation (v. 8).

V. 7 has been thought to refer to Gethsemane. In what way was this prayer of Jesus heard? Not by the removal of the cup of suffering, but rather through his exaltation (cf., the fourth servant song) in which he was designated as High Priest.

The Episcopal and Pres./UCC/Chr. Ch. readings (Hebrews 10) contain the crucial passage (vv. 5-10) to which we have already alluded as the quintessential definition of what is meant when we speak of Jesus' death as a sacrifice, viz., a life of total commitment in obedience to the will of God, culminating in death. The Episcopal reading, which runs through v. 25, goes beyond the doctrinal exposition to the exhortation (vv. 19-25), urging the baptized worshipers (v. 22b) to "draw near" (a cultic word), to love and do good works, and not to neglect assembling together for liturgical purposes.

*Gospel: John 18:1—19:42 (John 19:17-30).* The passion narrative of the Fourth Gospel begins at 18:1. Here the Johannine style exhibited in discourses couched in typically Johannine language is abandoned for a straightforward narrative. Only in a few places (e.g., in the trial before Pilate with its dialogue about truth, John 18:36-38), is there an echo of distinctive Johannine themes. It is probable that John's passion narrative represents a distinct and independent tradition from those of the synoptists. We will note here some of its distinctive features. It is remarkably well oriented on the topography of Jerusalem (Kidron, the praetorium, Gabbatha), and history (Annas as the power behind the high priestly throne). More primitive, too, is the absence of Jesus' prayer in Gethsemane, the self-identification of Jesus with the coming Son of man at the investigation before the high priest (18:19). Also its chronology is more plausible (the dating of the crucifixion on the eve of the Passover, rather than on the day itself, 19:14). On the other hand, later apologetic is at work in the participation of the temple police in the arrest. There are legendary features, such as the naming of Malchus and Peter (18:10), the episode between the mother of Jesus and the beloved disciple, which perhaps has allegorical significance, as does the omission of the breaking of the legs (identifying Jesus with the passover lamb) and the story of the lance and the outflow of water and blood, symbolizing perhaps the gospel sacraments. The overall effect of the Johannine passion narrative is to stress the glory of Jesus in the midst of his passion. Note how at every point Jesus remains master of the situation. See, for instance, the arrest (18:5-10), Jesus' behavior before the high priest (18:23), and finally Jesus' making his own will and deciding himself on the moment of his death (v. 30). He dies with the triumphant cry, *consummatum est* (19:30). The weakness of the RSV (KJV), "it is finished," is unpardonable.

The Pres./UCC/Chr. Ch. lectionary again goes its own way, following the Lucan passion (Luke 23:33-46). It thus opts for the least theological, though most affecting, of the passion stories, the one which has transposed the passion from the key of tragedy to the key of pathos (Dibelius). This transposition is shown in the three Lucan words from the cross. First, there is Jesus' prayer, "Father, forgive them" (the omission of these words, noted in the RSV margin, is apparently due to later antisemitism). Second, the episode of the penitent and impenitent thieves, which looks like a homiletic elaboration of the earlier tradition that both the thieves railed on Jesus. Third, the last word, from Ps. 31:5, the Jewish bedtime prayer, instead of Ps. 22:1. Then there is the substitution of "this man was an innocent man," for the more theologically motivated confession of the Marcan centurion, "Truly this was the Son of God." But perhaps Luke was closer to history in attributing the darkness to an eclipse. In Mark it is supernatural and a piece of eschatological symbolism. The overall tone of the Lucan passion narrative is the culmination of the life of the gracious savior who goes out in love to others.

## HOMILETICAL INTERPRETATION

Today's readings, except for the Pres./UCC/Chr. Ch., appear at first glance to put the homilist in something of a bind. If he follows the indications in the first two readings, then he may develop the theme of Jesus as the man of sorrows, as one who shared our humanity in every way, who was tempted and experienced weakness, especially the great weakness of man, the fear of death; and yet in the midst of his dying he showed that fear of death may be overcome by one who is firmly rooted in hope.

If, on the other hand, he chooses to follow the indications of the Gospel according to John, then he will be singing the victory of Jesus over all the forces that opposed him. In John's account Jesus is always the master of every situation.

This picture seems at variance with the first, or at least seems to put the homilist in the position of having to establish two quite distinct moods. Perhaps approaching John's Gospel from a certain viewpoint will bring the readings into harmony.

First of all, the homilist has at his disposal one of the most powerfully moving passages ever composed. In fact, the language of the fourth servant song is so extraordinary and so easily grasped by the listener, the homilist would do well to make his comments prior to the reading of this selection. In that way he can prepare his hearers to receive its impact directly.

He should ask them to recognize that the church saw in the figure of the servant a prophetic description of Jesus: by his sufferings our sins have been taken away. The point of this is not for us to feel guilty or to try and work up some sense of shame. The servant is a hero who has won a great victory for us. We should rejoice and be grateful.

In the original meaning of the fourth servant song the Gentiles are the ones who despise the people of Israel and hold them of no account. And yet out of the sufferings of this people came salvation for the Gentiles: Who could believe it? It was to this lowly people that the power of Yahweh was revealed (cf. 53:1).

It is true that over the centuries we have continued to act as the Gentiles did, to look down on certain races and classes of people, to lay heavy burdens of suffering on them and then attribute their unhappy condition to a punishment inflicted on them by God.

Yes, we have a great deal to learn about the ways of God with man, but let us not fail to hear the glorious words of salvation which the fidelity of the servant has called forth: "on him lies a punishment that brings us peace, and through his wounds we are healed" (53:5).

The first reading in the Pres./UCC/Chr. Ch. lectionary must have special treatment. It directly pertains to a tragedy that befell Jerusalem and attributes this to her having sinned grievously. She laments the fact that her enemy has triumphed over her. This can be applied to the passion only with the greatest care. The final verse is very touching if placed on the lips of Jesus: "All you who pass this way, look and see: is any sorrow like the sorrow that afflicts me," but the remainder of the sentence makes it very inappropriate as attributed to Jesus: "[the sorrow] with which Yahweh has struck me on the day of his burning anger?" (Lam. 1:12).

To attribute these verses to the proper subject, Jerusalem, runs the risk of summoning up images of a wrathful God wreaking vengeance on Jerusalem for having crucified his Son Jesus. This is wholly alien to the spirit which moved Jesus during his passion, and it is from him that we learn the attitude of his Father; out of love he sent his Son into the world so that through his sacrifice all men might be saved.

The second readings continue the theme of Jesus as the man of sorrows. He has now come into his glory but the author of Hebrews is at pains to establish the permanent importance for us of how he got there. In Heb. 4:14—5:10 we are told that Jesus deserves to be *our* high priest because he fully shares our humanity. To put it more precisely, he was so subject to the condition of being human that he was tempted in every way that we are. The author is not thinking of the three temptations by Satan in the desert at the beginning of his public life. Jesus was subjected to the test throughout his ministry, but especially at the end of his life.

We are not presented with the masterful Jesus of the Fourth Gospel here. No, we see rather a Jesus struggling against his weakness, especially before the prospect of his being handed over to be put to death. He is a Jesus who cries aloud and who sheds silent tears, praying to the one who had the power to save him out of death.

Having learned obedience in the school of suffering, he is acclaimed by God with the title of high priest, but he remains *our* high priest. In his glory he has the power to bring us to salvation, but he reached that state by struggling with his weakness. He remembers what it is to be tested. He is a high priest who can sympathize with our weakness. In our need we can turn to him in perfect confidence that he will reach out to us with compassion.

In Heb. 10:1-25 the power of our high priest to save us is described. In contrast to the old sacrifices that needed to be repeated again and again, we learn that the perfect obedience of Jesus has given all of us access to the Father. Because he hoped in God, we too may have hope.

A most dramatic example of Jesus' hope is in the Gospel selection from the Pres./UCC/Chr. Ch. lectionary. Jesus is being mocked and jeered at as he hangs nailed to the cross. If he has any power, now is the time to use it—on his own behalf. The leaders of the people, the Roman soldiers, even one of the criminals hanging beside him, all urge him in mocking tones to save himself.

Something in us urges him also to pop the nails from his hands and feet, and by his show of strength to confound his enemies and give comfort to his grieving followers. But he has no power to come down from the cross. Unless his Father acts, and acts quickly, he will pass into the darkness of death with the mocking cries still being hurled at him, the derisive epilogue that sums up the failure of his mission.

Abandoned, powerless, alone, on the point of death, Jesus still clung fast to his hope in God. Luke writes: "when Jesus had cried out in a loud voice, he said, 'Father, into your hands I commit my spirit' " (Luke 23:46, citing Ps. 31:5).

When we turn to the Gospel according to John the atmosphere is in many respects quite different. In the garden of Gethsemane there is no mention of an agony scene. Instead Jesus is presented as "knowing everything that was going to happen to him" (18:4). The soldiers who come to arrest him fall to the ground at the mention of his name (v. 6). Jesus directs them to arrest him and let the disciples go (v. 8). In the dialogues with Caiaphas and with Pilate Jesus is clearly in command. In fact, it is established that he is a king (v. 37). He speaks three times from the cross: once it is to commit his mother to the care of the beloved disciple; the second time he says, "I am thirsty," and John notes the reason is to fulfill the scripture perfectly (v. 28); finally Jesus proclaims the victory, "It is accomplished" and gives up his spirit (v. 30).

John, of course, is aware of Jesus' sufferings, but is pointing out that the same events viewed with the eyes of faith may be transformed from a seeming defeat into a glorious exaltation. It may indeed be the supreme revelation of God to man in Jesus. John uses a number of images to describe the climactic moments of Jesus' life. The passion is conceived as Jesus' return to the Father, a gracious way to describe the suffering and death Jesus was to undergo. John begins his account of the Last Supper with the solemn words that "Jesus knew that the hour had come for him to pass from this world to the Father" (John 13:1). Again he notes that Jesus knew that "he had come from God and was returning to God" (John 13:3).

A second image which John uses to refer to the crucifixion/resurrection/ascension is that of being "lifted up." The first step in his return to the Father is his being lifted up on the cross. Just as Moses lifted up a bronze serpent in the desert, so, Jesus said, the Son of man must be lifted up in order that each one who believes in him may possess eternal life (cf. John 3:13-15). Jesus will be recognized then as having divine rank: "when you have lifted up the Son of man, then you will know that I am he" (John 8:28). The effect of his being lifted up on the cross will be so powerful and so magnificent as to make men forget its original grim appearance: "And when I am lifted up from the earth, I shall draw all men to myself" (John 12:32).

A third image is taken from the language of royalty, but John employs it in his own special way. The Jesus who is proclaimed "King of the Jews" by Pilate and by the Roman soldiers is indeed a king. His crown, though, is a crown of thorns and he is dressed in a rough purple robe. He is slapped and whipped and finally nailed to a cross and, strangely enough, this is what reveals him to be a king: "Yes," he says to Pilate, "I am a king. For this was I was born and for this I came into the world: to bear witness to the truth" (John 18:37). So it was that when Pilate handed Jesus over to be crucified he had a notice fixed to the cross. The notice was written in Hebrew, Latin, and Greek so that all men would be able to identify this man, "Jesus of Nazareth, King of the Jews."

These lines on the kingship of Jesus are heavy with irony. A pagan governor confers the title on him. The chief priests and the people reject it. None of them understands what kind of king Jesus really was.

Today a homilist may be tempted to avoid the title altogether. Royalty has fallen to a very low estate in our day. The external trappings remain but a monarch no longer rules alone. Even if a homilist should re-create for his congregation the former glory of the king, he then must face the problem that Jesus was not that kind of king. And yet there is something about that title. Even today it speaks to something deep in us, a longing that no earthly king could ever respond to. We may at times thrill to the sight of a magnificent king who rules with power from a mighty palace. But our heart yearns for another kind of leader, one who is close to us and shares our life and who calls forth from us, not awe, but love.

Luke seems to have caught this aspect of the kingdom of Christ perfectly in his description of the good thief, contained in the Pres./UCC/Chr. Ch. lectionary for today. As Jesus is hanging on the cross, he is mocked by those about him. If he is the man he says he is, then he ought to save himself. This challenge is hurled at him by the leaders of the people (Luke 23:35), by the Roman soldiers (v. 37) and finally by one of the criminals crucified with him (v. 39). But the other thief surprisingly takes Jesus' part, then turns to Jesus and says, "Jesus, remember me when you come into your kingdom" (v. 42). Older translations had him saying, "*Lord*, remember me," but that misses the whole point. He does not see a "Lord." He sees only Jesus, and yet somehow he knows that Jesus cannot save himself. The thief understands that Jesus is a very special kind of king and asks to be with him in that kingdom.

A fourth image used to express this mysterious revelation of God in Jesus is found in John's use of the term "glory." The first events of the passion itself are referred to as the beginning of Jesus' glorification: "Father, the hour has come. Glorify your Son in order that the Son may glorify you" (John 17:1).

It is not simply the case that John is too sensitive a spirit and so is unable to face the harsh reality of Jesus' passion. He is sensitive but in a different sense of the word. He is not simply anticipating the splendor of the resurrection in order to brighten up the gloom of the crucifixion. John is saying that the glory of God shines magnificently through all the events of the passion for those with eyes to see.

This same glory of God accompanies his manifestations throughout the OT. When God gave Israel the Ten Commandments, the glory of Yahweh settled on Mount Sinai and "to the eyes of the sons of Israel the glory of Yahweh seemed like a devouring fire on the mountain top" (Exod. 24:17). This glory is the radiance, the epiphany to men, of God's majesty, his power and his holiness.

All these mighty attributes are also revealed in the passion of Jesus but in a strikingly different way. John does not view the cross simply as a stage that Jesus must pass through so that the glory of God may then appear, i.e., what we would recognize as glory. John is saying that in the very suffering of Jesus the glory of God appears, or better, in his passion Jesus is revealing to us God himself.

From this point of view John's account does not seem so much at variance in spirit with the first two readings. God's glory is manifested in the weakness of Jesus and in his strength, in his humiliation and in his exaltation, in his fear of dying and in his unshakable conviction that it was into God's hands that he was handing over his spirit.